dear beautiful friend,

Edited by Freydis Lova.
Cover design by Rachel Clift.
Book design & layout by Rachel Clift.
rcliftpoetry.com

First printing edition, 2023.

Sara Christiansen
@dearbeautifulfriend

dear beautiful friend,

BY

SARA CHRISTIANSEN

For my grandmothers, Adele and Chris,
whose love & light I will carry with me always.

Dear friend,

I hope wherever you are, whatever journey you're on, and whatever you're going through today, that as you read these words, you are able to pause for a moment and let this truth sink in:

You are beautiful.
Mind, body, and soul.
Every part of you and each version of you.
Past you, present you, future you.
In every hidden place, every scar, every battle wound, and every piece that may feel shattered.

And I want to remind you of this if you feel uncertain, afraid, lost, hopeless, or heart-broken, if you're struggling with confidence, if you're facing really hard things, or if you don't even have the words to describe your experience.

You are *brave*, because even when you feel fear, you keep courageously showing up as you are.

You may be deeply *hurting* today, but you are whole.

You are *worthy*, and so deserving of love.

You are *healing*, and growing, right here and now.

And you are still *shining* with a light that this world really needs.

I hope this book feels like a gentle pep talk from a friend who believes in you, is rooting for you, and understands, if even just a little, how you feel. I hope it reminds you of your immeasurable worth, how much you have to be proud of, and how far you have come, even if you can't see it right now. And I hope you know that it's okay to feel everything you're feeling, that there are brighter days waiting for you, and most of all, that you are not alone.

Thank you for being beautifully *you*.

Love,
Sara Christiansen

CONTENTS

dear brave friend,

dear beautiful, *brave* friend,

This struggle won't last indefinitely,
and when it comes to an end,
and you're standing on top
of the mountain peak,
you'll be amazed at how
you pushed through uncertainty and fear,
and the things that don't make sense right now
will become so much more clear.

perfect balance

You are a beautiful blend
of bravery and tenderness.
Please don't ever let anyone
make you feel
like you're any less.

the smallest steps

It can be tempting to keep looking back

when this moment right here feels unsure,

but remember all you overcame to get to this day-

how you rose up with strength and endured.

Beautiful friend, you can do it again

when you feel like you have nothing left.

Just keep breathing,
hold on,
and remember-

the biggest victories come from the smallest of steps.

You might feel weak,

like all your strength is drained,

but please don't underestimate

the tremendous courage that it takes

to keep showing up day after day.

Even though you feel afraid,
you're doing it anyway.
That is so incredibly brave
no matter what self-doubt may say.

through it all

It might feel really scary right now–
like that pit in your stomach won't go away.
You've taken a leap into the great unknown,
but now you're wondering if it will all be okay.
Please trust yourself here in this moment.
You followed your heart and that's a beautiful thing,
and although you wish you could see into the future,
remember the gifts that uncertainty can bring–

It makes you hang on tighter to the present.
It makes you treasure the small victories.
And if you let it, it will teach you freeing surrender
as you learn to stop searching for guarantees.
Please don't second guess your heartfelt decisions.
Don't devalue your instincts, or be afraid to fall
because these truths will never ever leave you–

You are *brave*.

You are *loved*.

And you will *grow through it all*.

beauty

You're trying
with every step you take.

You're not quitting
or sitting in mistakes.

You're still breathing,
and although you feel unsure,
you have the strength to endure
the harshest storm,
the coldest winter,
the hole you feel you're sinking in,

although you're worn,
although you falter,
you still have untold power within,

you won't let the fear win,

and beauty is emerging from all that's been.

You are enough
right now
right here
and love wraps you in its arms
and holds you near

may the truth of this moment
overshadow your fear

may the stumbling blocks and obstacles
begin to disappear
and although you feel the valid pain
and sting of many tears
I hope you remember the power you have
and the strength to persevere.

legacy

You're feeling everything deeply
and refusing a disguise

you value truth over appearance
and although the overwhelm is high

the roots that formed
through this great storm

so deep
                   and strong
                                   and wide

are growing something pure and real
that will last for all of time.

be held

Things that hold you tight
on your hardest, longest night:

love

hope

grace

truth

and most of all
your future self
that bravely made it through.

(your future self is so proud of you today)

brave

Beautifully,

remarkably,

authentically,

vulnerably,

embracing growth.

Look at you,
showing up and brave,
healing, whole,
breathing in today.

Look at you,
persisting through
what wasn't easy–
but you stayed true.

Look at you,
further down the road
with dreams fulfilled,
and love that flows.

Look at you,
in every stage–
you learned, you grew
and overcame.

co-existing

The way you are taking things in stride
still hoping and dreaming
along with the tears you've cried,

watching pain and fear and joy and hope
existing side by side,

is giving me the strength
to make it through
and keep reaching for the light.

There will be people who want to see you fall
and people who want to see you fly.

There will be times you want to give your all
and times you want to run and hide.

There will be days you're soaring with the birds
and days you're crashing with the waves,

but you'll hold space for love even when you hurt
and that is the very definition of brave.

It's heavy, I know,
and it's not how you thought
it would turn out at all.

The progress feels slow,
and you're tired of trying
to rise after each fall.

But look how you glow–
this phenomenal wonder of strength
makes your soul stand so tall

The beautiful bravery you show–
when courage knocks on your door,
you keep answering the call.

spring

inhale

exhale

hang on in the hardest hour

then look above the soil

for the first budding flower

Future you
will be so proud
of the way
you're showing up right now.

the tree

You may feel stranded,
unnourished,
not knowing
when you'll emerge
from the senseless night,
but I see you
beautifully planted,
flourished,
growing,
soaked in endless,
radiant light.
And when you're overwhelmed
by all that could not be,
and by all that's still yet to come,
remember how the sun shines upon the tree
and heals the memory
of what winter has undone.

Its branches, though worn,
have miraculously
endured another shadowy frost,
and it's stronger now
with deeper roots
for the multitude of leaves
that it has lost.

And you, my friend,
are stronger too,
and the richness of your journey
can shelter those in time of need
and remind them of their worth and beauty.

Sometimes leaving the path you are on is

the wisest decision, and the key to finding incredible

opportunities that are waiting, because you didn't let fear

prevent you from pursuing a new direction.

It's not too late to start again
if the path you're on doesn't feel right.
And it can be scary to be a beginner,
trying to find your way through the lonely night,
but there's room and there's time to change your mind
if that's where your heart is leading you.
There's courage and freedom in becoming unstuck
and shifting direction when you need to.
Uncertainty can hold a special kind of beauty
that's only discovered as you venture out,
just remember, you hold untold strength within you–

you have everything you need right here and now.

Some things that are brave about you

It's brave the way you keep showing up as your authentic self.

It's brave the way you take another small step forward.

It's brave the way you rest when you need to.

It's brave the way you keep your heart soft and open,
even though you've been hurt.

It's brave the way you give yourself compassion
when you're struggling.

It's brave the way you keep learning and growing.

It's brave the way you hope,

the way you heal,

the way you dream,

and the way you love with such a deep capacity.

You're one step closer to the future you can see.

One breath deeper into all that's meant to be.

One rung higher on the climb to victory.

work of art

Don't ever be ashamed of who you are-
not your journey,
        your setbacks,
        or any of your scars.
They all form the canvas,
                        the colors,
                                the stars
        that make your life a rare work of art.

the uprising

In the uprooting
and the undoing

in the unlearning
and the uprising

you are growing
you are hoping
you are reaching for new horizons

and soon will come the day
when you will stand, wild and brave
and share the wisdom that you've gained
with someone else who is afraid

they'll see the fire in your eyes
and it will give them strength to try

they'll believe that they can fly
because you refused a false disguise
instead you felt the pain and fear and love and joy

and held on tight.

dear hurting friend,

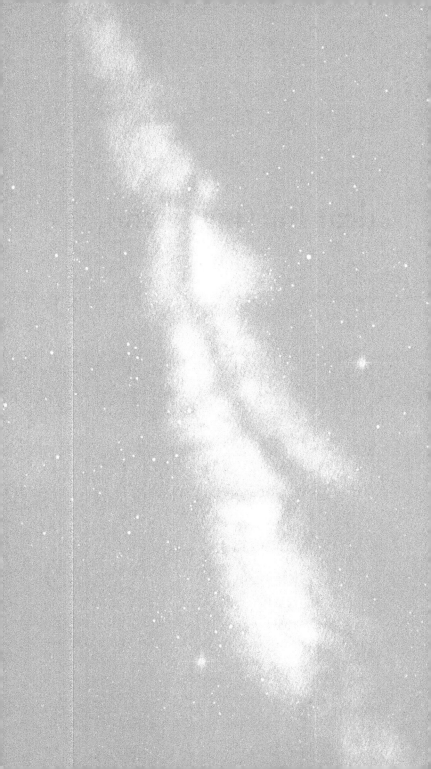

dear beautiful friend with a broken heart,

I hope you feel
with every passing moment
that your heart is getting stronger,
and I hope you find the grace today
to hang on a little longer.

transcending

You didn't sign up for this
you don't know how to make it through
and you absolutely do not deserve
pain of this magnitude

but it is not hopeless

there is more to your story than this

there's glory on the other side of this

and until you get there,
may you find right here
an extra dose of hope and comfort
as companions to your tears
and may you look back
in days, months, and years
and see how transcending love
overcame your deepest fears.

healing balm

If you're going through a hard season,
I hope you know you're not alone,
and I hope one day soon you will look back
and see how much you've courageously grown.

All you have to do right now,
is breathe in grace and breathe out fear,
and know that better days are waiting,
no matter how huge this moment appears.

Just think of all the times before,
when you overcame what you never thought you could,
and how you survived to tell the story
of the many storms of life you withstood.

Although it doesn't feel like it right now,
these relentless winds will calm,
and the love you've acquired and the wisdom you've gained
will pour out of your heart like a healing balm.

the shifting

one step at a time

one breath

one day

it's going to be alright

and you have the strength
that it takes

the sun is going to shine

and you'll see beauty from
all of the rain

and healing and wholeness and light
will shift the heartache and pain

What a beautiful heart you have-
and if right now it's torn in two,
remember that beautiful hearts can heal
and love will never let go of you.

I hope the mirror reflects to you
the light you hold inside,
and I hope that through your hardest night,
love will be your guide.

your best

Sometimes another step feels impossible,
like the walls are closing in on you,
your dreams eclipsed by your reality,
and you're too tired to keep pushing through.

I hope you give yourself permission
to just breathe deep,
to sink into grace
and get some rest.
This life is not a pass or fail test-

*it's abundantly enough
that you're trying your best.*

in time

Please know that you are being guided
by a force of love that's sometimes hard to see

especially when your days feel like constant struggle
and you're no longer sure what to believe

the pain you've been through is not in vain
and there will be an end to this difficult climb

the work you're doing and the seeds you're sewing
will produce something beautiful in their time.

You are worthy of receiving
the same love that you give away.

You are worthy of believing
you're not defined by what they say.

Doubt and fear can be deceiving
and make you feel like you've lost your way,

but the path you are on is truly leading
to a brighter, better, hopeful day.

human

Sometimes you might wish you didn't care so much
because then the pain wouldn't be as deep,
but your caring and what feels like
the breaking of your heart
is a sign of its vast capacity,
and that is a beautiful thing,
even when it hurts-
especially when it hurts-
because it shows how much love
you are capable of,
and the love that is within you,
that is causing you to feel this ache right now,
is the same love
that will guide and heal you,
and never leave you.
That love is yours forever-
it's intertwined with the deepest parts of you.

What a lovely
loving
healing
deeply-feeling
human you are.

The fight might be draining you,
but you have what it takes
to make it through.
Please know you're not a burden
and you're not weak-
you are *exactly* the kind of light
that this world needs.

feel all the colors

If you're feeling off today
and not like you, or lost your way,
like you're floating in a strange abyss,
please know it won't always be like this.

You're stronger than you think you are,
and braver than you thought you'd be-
it's okay to see the clouds
and lose sight of the shore in the endless sea.

I hope you remember you're not alone,
and just as you are, you're valued and loved.
One day soon you'll find your way home
and soak in the sun and its warmth from above.

So feel all the colors, and all of their ranges,
and know that when one is on brighter display,
the others are still there, they haven't gone anywhere,

and they will shine again on another day.

You are fury
and wonder
and light
and you have the strength it takes
to get through this night.

clarity

I hope today, if just for a moment,
the clouds roll back and the fog disappears.

I hope the loneliness rests awhile
and you're able to exhale some of the fear.

I hope you close your eyes and lift your head,
feeling the sun's warmth on your face,
and that your heart fills with anticipation
as you breathe in unconditional grace.

I hope you magically catch a glimpse
of the good things that are in store,
and that you see a little of your future
with dreams come true and open doors.

I hope it gives you strength to continue,
even though you might feel tired and drained,

and I hope one day you'll tell the story
of how you found beauty in the middle of pain.

Keep looking up
while you're walking through this valley-
even among shadows
there's so much light to see.

May you know today
and never forget
that your story
isn't nearly finished yet

maybe you're in
a really hard chapter
but this overwhelming part
will not last forever

the struggle will ease
and the pages will turn
and reveal new paragraphs
with wonderful words

right now might feel long,
relentless,
unbending,
but hold onto the hope of a beautiful ending.

you are not hard to love

It causes so much pain to absorb
someone else's unhealed projection
and then think that it's somehow a reflection
of how lovable and worthy and good you are.

If anyone made you feel like you're hard to love,
please take that thought and throw it far,
because you were born with a beautiful soul

you are wonderful,

wise,

gifted,

and whole

and your life and presence right here matters,
I hope you remember this when your heart feels shattered-
some of your best memories and moments are ahead,
and you will find the right people who treasure you instead.

Sometimes savoring the journey
is an impossibility,
a fantasy,
a task that's too great to ask.

How do you savor pain,
days of endless rain,
and loss eclipsing gain?

How do you endure sorrow
and keep singing of tomorrow?

How do you see light
when you can't see the end?
How do you have hope
that your heart will ever mend?

But you're *feeling*
and that's no small thing.
You're *breathing*,
and right now,
somehow,
you're *still believing*
that love is weaving
better days up ahead.

It might not feel like it
but that's enough-
clinging to the vision of the smooth
while swimming in the depths of the rough.
There's nothing else demanded of you,
nothing else you have to prove,
you have the ache for things to be better,
and you have the truth,

and beautiful friend,
that will surely guide you through.

hang on

What if everything comes together
after it all falls apart?

What if wholeness happens
beyond the shattering of a heart?

What if beauty blossoms
and replaces all the weeds?

What if purpose blooms
in what could never be?

What if hope displaces
the looming nagging doubts?

What if sunshine rises
and silver lines the clouds?

What if love wins everything
and time helps with the wounds?

What if every misplaced step
led me straight to you?

What if together, we could change
the darkness into light
and find what's true and brave and good—
what if it's worth the fight?

If I could give you anything,
it would be the love and strength
to breathe another breath right now,
and hang on another day—
then I'd hold up a mirror
and show you what I see:

a precious diamond shining bright,
a gem that this world needs.

the gift of today

The pause and the stillness
can be disconcerting
when you're feeling lost
and your heart is hurting,
but it's okay to soak in those moments-
to just be
and to breathe
and to take in the seconds

remind the uncertainty
that it can have space

remind the fear and doubt
that they have a safe place

and the past can rest awhile,
the future can wait-
there's still hope to be found
in the gift of today.

It might feel gray right now,

but you haven't lost your way.

There's still endless light within you,

and soon you'll feel the warmth of day.

hope

heroic

optimism

profoundly

enduring

Just a little reminder
after all you've been through–
holding onto hope is a miracle,
and beautiful soul, *so are you.*

you're not alone

To the beautiful friend
who is struggling to believe
that things are working
and aligning behind the scenes,
I'll hold enough hope
for both of us today
and I know that if
I ever lose my way,
you'll hold hope
for both of us too,
and over and over,

we'll make it through.

Your story isn't finished,
and your worth can't be diminished.
Keep believing this is true-
there's so much more in front of you.

phenomenal

If you feel like you're running on empty,
    and exhausted from heartache and pain,
        and you keep looking for silver linings,
            but all you find is more rain-

If your hope is all frayed at the edges,
    and your strength is a thing of the past,
        and you're tired of positive platitudes,
            and your patience is thinning out fast-

I hope that these words will remind you
    it's okay to feel like you do-
        you don't have to perform to be worthy
            or pretend that the sky is all blue.

I hope you can stop and remember
    how courageous you've been to get here.
        I hope you celebrate each little step
            you took despite any fear.

Your genuine heart has propelled you,
    no part of your journey's a waste,
        healing and growth aren't linear,
            and you deserve compassion and grace.

I hope that along with the struggle
    you also find moments of rest,
        and that you are able to see who you are-

        a phenomenal human who's doing their best.

You might not be able to see it right now,

but all of those beautiful seeds you are sewing,

all of those brave steps you are taking,

all of the love and kindness you are spreading,

all of the hope you are choosing,

all of the progress you are making,

and all of the things you are learning-

all *matter*,

nothing is wasted,

and it's bringing you closer to the

audacious, stunning

vision you have for your life.

dear worthy friend,

I hope today
you understand
a little more
that your worth is greater
than every grain of sand
that scatters on the shore.

I hope today you know
how loved you are,
more than all the galaxies,
the moon,
the sun,
and stars.

three wishes

I wish we could get rid of the word perfection.

I wish we could redefine the word broken.

I wish that every time you look at your reflection,
you hear the words that truth has spoken,
and you see love staring back at you,
holding you,
helping you make it through,
showing you the magnitude
of strength and sunlight you possess,
and that your eyes will smile
and your heart will rest.

worthy

Whole and complete just as you are;

one of a kind, and deserving of

radical love and belonging

that forever ignites your

heart with the magnitude of

your indisputable value.

You belong-
and you have all along.
There are glorious notes
only you can bring to the song.

You are worthy

        incredible

         majestic

          and strong

(anyone who tries to say otherwise is wrong).

be held

You are a bright light
that illuminates the darkest night,
and although you may be feeling
exhausted from the fight,
you're still persevering
with all of your might

so today you can rest and let love hold you tight.

No matter what anyone says about you,
the essence of who you are
and the beauty of your heart
will keep shining through.

When fear shouts
there's no way out

and shame pretends
that it has clout

if hope has shriveled
in the drought

please don't doubt
what you're about-

love
and light
within
without.

in case you forgot

To the beautiful human
exhausted from breaking,
trying to fit into spaces
that leave you empty and aching,
who feels labeled, dismissed
misjudged or unheard,
whose forgotten your magic
and can't see your worth,
I hope you remember
this unshakable truth-

you're enough

you belong

exactly as you.

Just a reminder to:
relax your shoulders
lift your chin
remember the power you have within-

an internal compass
that knows the next step
when you quiet the noise
and take a deep breath

forget everything that
they told you to be
and all the times
you felt unworthy

all you have to do
is keep being you
keep going, keep dreaming
(and rest when you need to).

empathy

Everyone shares a collective humanity,

making us deeply connected even when our

paths are different-

and that is a beautiful thing that deserves a wholehearted effort

to understand the experience of another as if it

happened to

you.

What you may have been told is a weakness
is really a rare delicate flower-
a sensitive soul watered with tenderness
makes empathy *your superpower.*

your wildest dreams

You are loved

you are known

you are seen

and you have something truly unique
that this world needs

I hope *I am worthy*
becomes your heartfelt creed

and that you see so many flowers
from your persevering seeds

I hope that wholeness draws you near
and holds you at the seams

and that you feel complete beyond
your biggest, wildest dreams.

Still waters run deep may be
a way to describe you,
but remember, beautiful friend,

that is a force of nature too.

You don't deserve anything less
than a true reciprocation
of the love you have in your heart
and a deep appreciation
of the beautiful person you are.

I hope one day soon
you feel overwhelmed
in the best possible way
by the love you receive,
after all the times you gave
much more than
you got in return,
after all the times your heart ached
and you forgot what you're worth.
I hope each of your beautiful wishes come true,
and I hope wonderful things happen for you.

You are one in a universe of billions

and loved just as you are

your heart is whole and compassionate

and you shine like the brightest of stars

don't let anyone convince you otherwise

their words don't hold any truth

they can't change your incredible value

you are beautifully, wonderfully you.

You are worthy of a new start.

You are worthy of healing for your broken heart.

You are worthy of believing that you are enough.

You are worthy of true belonging and unconditional love.

Please don't let their voices
occupy the space
that was only meant for love and grace.

exactly as you are

Maybe there are times you thought
you'd be further along by now.
Some days can feel like you're lost in defeat,
stuck on repeat
with no clear way to get out.

But please don't think for one minute
that love has ever left you,
and please don't believe for one second
that you won't make it through,
even when it all feels like too much
and like what you're doing just isn't enough,
remember that your life and your light are still shining,
and there is growth even with pain and fear colliding.

There is more than how it seems in this moment,
there's a door open and waiting for you-
it's filled with hope and healing
and the beautiful truth:

You are love,
you are loved,
exactly as you are.

Even when the sky is dark,
you're the shining star,
and it's worth celebrating today
that you have come so far.

You are love,
you are loved,
exactly as you are.

When you feel lost in a sea of people,
and trapped in comparison's walls,
and you can't remember the last time
you felt secure, or knew who you were at all,
may you remember your genuine beauty,
your strength and your sincerity,
and may you know with deepest certainty,
that you are *always worthy.*

You belong in every space
your heart calls you to,
don't let anything they say
convince you it's not true.

extraordinary

Please remember
you don't have to be
more of this, or more of that,
and you don't need to
exhaust yourself
trying to wear all the different hats.
Maybe you've heard this
hundreds of times,
but today, let it really sink in-
you are unique
and you are enough:
a beautiful, extraordinary human.

There are not enough

      words in the world,

      or stars in the sky,

      peaks upon mountains,

      or birds flying high,

to compare with your worth

and the way that you shine-

you're an infinite wonder

unique, and divine.

You are worthy of

(beautiful
plentiful
reciprocal
unequivocal
caring
soul-baring
invested
time-tested
sunshine and rain
unashamed
professing
no second guessing
validating
unabating)

love.

I hope when you walk into
the spaces your heart is calling you to,
you feel the warmth and light
you are so deserving of.

I hope as you step out and press forward
despite the fear you feel,
you are met with a calm
that empowers you to keep going.

I hope in the hidden places
where their hurtful words still lodge,
you heal so completely that it becomes
harder and harder to recall what they said.

I hope the overwhelming uncertainty
that engulfs you at times,
is eclipsed by the gentle intuition
that has guided you again and again.

I hope when you catch a glimpse of your reflection,
the truest voice that tells you you're beautiful
drowns out the critic
that would try to tell you otherwise.

I hope when you get to the end of today,
you are able to breathe deeply,
celebrate your magic,
and remember how far you have come.

dear healing friend,

Healing takes time-
it's tender and can't be rushed,
but the sun will once again shine
and mend the parts of you that feel crushed.
The shattered pieces can re-align
and form something more beautiful than before-
a stunning, wild design,
a place where endless light pours,
where hope is restored,
and fear can't win anymore.

lost and found

Sometimes we lose hope
and that's okay,
it miraculously has a way
of finding us again.

Please know it's not all how it seems.
Things are working together behind the scenes-
stitch by stitch, this tapestry of dreams,
with every broken piece reinforced at the seams.

You are not behind where you're meant to be-
you haven't missed your future or your destiny.
The shattering is enriching your empathy,
and the waiting is preparing your story.

It may be taking all you have
just to take another step,
and making you exhausted
just to breathe another breath,

but beautiful things can blossom from the depths
(even when it doesn't look like it yet).

detour

Diverts you from your plans unexpectedly, but it can

end up being

this wonderful

opportunity to embrace what is beyond your control, and to

use the new path to find beauty

right where you are.

the waiting

Even in this moment of waiting
and not knowing what comes next,
there's beauty and wholeness and healing
to be found in each breath and each step.
Moments of new admiration
and noticing facets of light,
reflections in puddles
and gentle melodies
and the stillness that comes with the night.
And although this pause is beyond your control
and joy can feel threatened by fear,
one thing is clear in this vast unknown
there's goodness right now and right here.

my wish for you

May the things that tried to take from you
be the things that lead you to wholeness.
May the things that tried to shake the core of you
be the things that produce calm and stillness.
May the things that tried to displace you
be the things that truly make you
more courageous, and tender inside,
more curious, and more resolved to try.

May every tear you've cried
and every piece that shattered,
every untold wound
and each time you've felt battered
lead you to a deeper peace,
lead you to a better place
with the help you need along the way
guiding you at a perfect pace.

May you never feel alone,
and may you always know
that mountaintops await,
transcending valleys deep below,
and your struggle isn't wasted,
not one ounce of pain you've tasted
or cost you've had to pay
is ever lost in the journey you're on today.

gentle

You see that beautiful soul in the mirror?
Please don't be so hard on her.
She's fought some battles and climbed some hills,
and still she's here, after all she's endured.

You don't have to compare her to a made-up perfection
or a standard she feels like she can never achieve.
Instead, you can embrace that shining reflection
and pause, and attend to whatever she needs.

And at the end of today when she lies down to rest,
she'll thank you for treating her with care,
and she will be nourished by the tenderness
and the love and the grace that you have shared.

No matter what's been disrupted by fear,
abundant light still lives in you here,
and although the night seems long,
and like some hope has disappeared,
your shining resilience has never been more clear.

The pain wasn't for nothing.

The rejection can open new paths.

And the wisdom you're gaining is bigger
than the fear that tried to hold you back.

You're not defeated by this mountain.

You have what it takes to make the climb.

And even though you may have stumbled,

you'll arrive at the top in just the right time.

time out

breathe in and breathe out

and look up at the sky

this universe needs you

and your passion inside

but never at the cost

of your own peace of mind

it's okay to slow down

and take some much needed time

whenever you're ready

to take the next step

you'll be replenished

because you gave yourself rest

I hope you know
how *brave* it is
to follow your heart,
to chase your dreams,
to begin again,
to let yourself be seen.

I hope you know
how *strong* it is
to heal from the past,
to acknowledge the pain,
to get back up
again and again.

I hope you know
how *possible* it is
to find joy and purpose,
to reach your goals,
to rise from the ashes,
to believe that you're whole.

I hope you know
how *amazing* it is
to see you emerging
through this dark night,
and to be in a world
that's touched by your light.

What if today
you are kinder to yourself-
more gentle,
gracious,
forgiving,
and tender?

What if you water
the soil of hardship and challenge
with loving acknowledgement
of all you have overcome,
all you have withstood,
and all you have yet to achieve?

What if you surround yourself
with nourishment,
and cultivate wonder
in the smallest of moments?

What if you see progress
as the sum of your breaths
and the sum of your steps
when you felt like you couldn't
take even one more?

What if you sink deeply
into the notion
of release of shame,
and harsh words,
harsh actions
and reckless treatment of your heart?

Then maybe–
or most certainly–
you would rest
knowing you're doing your best.

You would heal
and allow yourself to feel.

You would soar
and find the beautiful things that are in store.

To the one who is desperately looking for answers
(but certainty keeps evading you),

I hope you find some rest today
and know that you will make it through.
It's normal for your mind to want to define
the blur and the mess you can't explain,
and feeling like if you knew why
would help to lessen all of the pain.
Please remember the light you carry inside
is brighter than the struggle you are in right now,
and the confusion you're feeling
won't stop you from healing,
and love will embrace the fear and doubt.

things to celebrate

I hope you know you have so much
to celebrate about yourself today,
like all the times you made it through
when you didn't think you had the strength,

and the times you learned and changed and grew
from your past and your mistakes,
how you're showing up and living brave
and giving every feeling space,

learning to accept all the parts of you
and letting go of fear and shame,
understanding that healing is a process
and you don't ever have to run from pain.

You're doing the work and trusting the timing,
believing that nothing you've been through is wasted,
and knowing one day you will see how things flourished
even in those uncertain times while you waited.

to do list

—Be gentle with your precious soul

—Remember that you're healing and whole

—Celebrate how much you have grown
        —the mountains you've climbed,
        —and the love that you've known

—Take some time to breathe and rest

—And don't forget that self-care is also progress.

You are healing
feeling deeply
letting go
and pushing through
and today I hope you find
the beauty that is waiting for you.

patience

Perpetually understanding that immediacy is not

always an option, and

tenaciously enduring the frustration of setbacks, without losing the

inspired hope that

each moment is teaching and preparing you, and

no amount of uncertainty and stillness is wasted;

compassionately caring for yourself in the waiting,

eventually seeing the dreams in your heart come to life.

(it will all be worth it, beautiful friend)

Maybe you've had to slow down without warning,
and right now is nothing like you expected it to be.
The night may feel long with no sign of morning
and the unlit road makes it hard to see.

Please remember that even in this time of waiting,
there is love and there is hope guiding your path,
and this uncertain season that you are enduring
will be clearer down the road when you look back.

I hope that soon you will see the horizon
ablaze with the most glorious sun,
and in that moment as your eyes widen,
you'll be amazed at how far you have come.

joy

Just embracing the goodness to be found in this moment,

offering

your inner child a chance to rest, play, and be free.

In the quiet uncertainty
and on the long twisting road,
you're finding joy in the most beautiful ways
and watching your purpose unfold.

I hope something incredible
happens to you today,
like a love note from life
that writes your fears away,
and reminds you to cherish
your inherent worth,
and what you and your good heart wholly deserve.
I hope that your dreams
come truly alive.
I hope that you heal
and I hope that you thrive.

Breathe,

feel,

hope,

heal,

repeat.

The possibilities are endless—
there's so much more
waiting for you.

The sun is rising again,

and you, my friend,
can rise again too.

dream

Daring to

reach for

every inspired,

alive imagination that

makes your soul spark.

Not everyone dreams your dreams-
but you do,
and there is a reason why.
So keep believing,
keep on going,

and watch how those dreams fly.

I hope you see a glimpse of your future
that rebuilds from all the scattered parts
and you watch yourself rising from burning ashes
with a purer, fiercer love in your heart.

What an incredible day it will be,
no matter how far away it may feel
when you're living, laughing, wild and free
and you realize the beautiful ways you have healed.

Just a little reminder
to be kind to yourself today-
you're doing your best,
and that's enough,
(and it's going to be okay).

I hope today you can rest
in knowing who you are.
No matter what came to stumble you,
you found your way through the dark,
and even though it hurt so deep
and there were times when you felt lost,
you anchored to your worth and light
and drew purpose from your loss.
I hope you know how brave that is,
and I hope you see your strength,
I hope your tomorrows bring healing
and I hope love fills all of your pain.

It's going to be so worth it.

all of the steps you're taking

all of the doors you've knocked on

all of the no's you've heard that have guided
your path in a new direction

all of the disappointment you've felt
when your plans were derailed

all of the times you've chosen what's true
over what others have expected of you

all of the unexpected detours
that felt beyond your control

all of the beliefs you've unlearned
that don't align with who you are

all of the moments you trusted yourself,
your instincts, and your good intentions

all of the beautiful reasons why you keep
pursuing the dreams in your heart.

the journey

Look how far you've come
since the beginning of this journey-
you've lived,
you've grown,
you've endured,
you've known
that fear doesn't have the final say
and hope shines on day by day,
and although you can't escape
the rain,
the thunder,
or the gray,
you've learned that joy exists with pain
and love is what remains.

dear shining friend,

I love how you shine
even in this hard time,
and I know it's not easy
for you to see,
but your light is still glowing
unconditionally.
It's okay to take the time you need
to rest,
to mend,
to heal,
to breathe.

And when you're ready to start again,
the sky will pause and hold its breath,
the stars will cheer and light the way,
the sun will rise higher on that day,
your heart will beat a little stronger,
and the earth will be left a whole lot brighter
because you'll keep spreading hope and love
and reminding people that they are enough.
You'll show them your battle scars
and your mended wounds,
you'll tell them that they
can make it through-

what a gift this world has in you.

Here is a gentle reminder for the week:
you are worthy
of the things that you seek,
but even if you never achieve
one more goal on your list,
you are enough
by just being you,
and this world is better
because you exist.

you're invited

There is always a place for you

no matter what you have been through

no matter who tries to uninvite you

there are no special hoops you have to jump through

no certain heights to measure up to

there's a seat at the table exactly for you

it's set beautifully and it's waiting for you

and no one else has the power to fill your shoes

may you know deep inside that this is true.

growing

It can be a lonely path sometimes,
and often, it's hard to see the light.
Life can hurt more than you realize,
and it's easy to feel overwhelmed
by the feelings inside.

But remember-

sunrise

fireflies

blue open skies

friends that are wise.

There's so much to hang onto
and so much to dispose,
but in it all and through it all,
there's still abundant hope.
There's truth and love and beauty-
even in the shadows.
The light and shade in everything
are there to hold you close,
until you feel
your sorrows fade
and acceptance overflows.
Then buds spring up in meadows,
you feel sand between your toes,
and day by day

you love

you live

you heal

you give

you grow.

Keep shining like you do–
this world really needs you.

authentic

Aiming for wholeness instead of perfection,

unapologetically pursuing what is

true, letting your

heart lead

every step of the way;

nuanced and grounded in compassion, and

trailblazing for

inclusivity and acceptance;

choosing substance over appearance.

Courageously being
the authentic,
true
version of you
gives others permission
to be themselves too.

I hope you can see your worth today

I hope you can feel it in a million ways

I hope it soaks in like the sun's glorious rays

I hope it leaves you in awe and amazed

I hope it lifts you for the rest of your days

and reminds you that no matter what anyone says,

the truth is you have just what it takes

to set this world ablaze.

You're resilient
and brilliant,
creative
and kind,

with a fierce, wild spirit
and a beautiful mind,

you are needed and loved,
sincere and courageous,

and the light that emits from your soul is contagious.

The love that you know

Through sleepless nights
and starlit wonder,
beneath endless rain
and roaring thunder,
up heavy hills
by winter's chill,
through painful tears
and forgotten years,
beyond judging glances and lonely dances,
and the worry that the dusk enhances,

still you're here
after all,

hope alive,
set mind,
standing tall,
heart wide,
eyes kind,
embracing all that came behind.

Piece by piece and step by step,
you reclaimed what you thought
was lost in the depths.
Breath by breath and stone by stone,
you found your way to North, to home.
And now as you reflect on the ways
that you've grown,
you see how you're ready for the places you'll go-
your story, your journey,
a beautiful show
of wholeheartedly living the love that you know.

song sheet

You count
you matter
you're known
you're seen

every step that you've taken
and everywhere that you've been
is a note in your song sheet–
a page in your history
bringing you to this day
and creating a way

for the world to hear what you have to say.

record setter

You fell a hundred times
in a hundred different ways.
You stumbled, tripped,
felt lost and sick,
overwhelmed by your lowest days.

You felt the pain,
you bled,
but you chose to rise instead.
It took every ounce of fight inside-
you overcame
and found your stride,
wiser from the tears you cried,

even then
you got back up again.

It didn't all go to plan,
sometimes it was so unfair,
but you kept on growing
and kept on going
to where only the wholehearted dare.

You changed direction when you needed to,
and learned to be still and rest.
You gave yourself compassion
at your worst and at your best.

You'd heard the word courageous before
but now you've lived each letter-
you've emerged with honors
and you're giving the tour;
you're a courageous record setter

(and your presence in the world makes this life so much better).

you are beautiful

Bravely accepting who you are and rejecting the mirage
of perfection, using
empathy as your superpower and living

authentically;

understanding that diversity comprises the

true richness of life,

inspiring others to embrace their uniqueness by your vulnerable,
fierce example and

uplifting presence;

loving yourself and humanity with genuine kindness.

I hope you feel seen today,
by the warmth of the sun
as it lights up your face,
by the tide as it washes
your heartaches away,
by the flowers in bloom
and the glow of the moon
but most of all
I hope you feel seen by you
as you celebrate the things
you've made it through,
as you remember your worth
with your dreams in clear view,
knowing wherever you go
and whatever you do,
you're a beautiful soul
holding fast to what's true.

reflection

I hope when you look at beauty,
you remember to see yourself too.

You may feel like you have
a long way to go,
a lot to unlearn,
and so much to know,
but today I hope
you can pause for a minute
to see how you've grown
and pushed past your limits.
Moment by moment,
you chose to keep going
when the winds came against you
and the current was flowing,
falling and rising,
with invisible horizons,
through sweat and tears,
with doubt and fear,
somehow, miraculously

you clung onto hope

and it returned your embrace,
and kept you afloat.
And just when you thought
you had no strength left to try,
the storm settled down
and the stars lit the sky.
You learned how to see
in the stillness of night,
and that breathing and resting
were essential to fight.

It's easy to forget
each mountain you've climbed,
and how you got back up
time after time,
but your heart is a witness-
front row and firsthand,
and the light you're emitting
writes on stone, not in sand:

Here is the life of a brave, wild soul,
knowing her worth,
healing and whole.
She may feel like she has
a long way to go,
a lot to unlearn,
and so much to know,
but as she reflects on her journey
and comes into her own,
today she will celebrate
how much she has grown.

You know that thing
that sets your soul on fire?
Remember to listen
to what it's telling you.
Those guideposts
made of your desires
are trustworthy,
wise,
and beautifully true.

Unashamed, brave
in the night and in the day
wildly, wholly embracing you

shaking off chains
healing from pain
feeling the light that is guiding you

up mountains
by valleys
on winding terrain
look how much you have made it through.

a toast to my beautiful friends

Here's to less fear
and always having laughter near.

Here's to learning and unlearning,
and burning away the old.

Here's to taking the shattered pieces
and turning them to gold.

Here's to building things that are new
and tearing down what's no longer true.

Here's to being fully in the moment,
to writing your story, and to bravely owning it.

Here's to embracing the joy and the pain in this life,
to great acts of kindness, and lifting each other high.

Here's to accepting and to letting go,
to slowing your pace and letting love flow.

Here's to unapologetically chasing dreams,
to doing the work, and resting with ease.

Here's to fun and to much-needed play,
to wonder and curiosity alive in every day.

And here's to hope, the most courageous act
that defies all the odds and holds nothing back.

Here's to tomorrow, to sunrise, to feeling at home,
and to knowing that you are never alone.

I'm so glad this book found you.
Thank you for reading these words.
Thank you for being beautifully you.

Love,
Sara Christiansen

SARA CHRISTIANSEN is a writer, Holistic Health Practitioner, and Certified Health and Wellness Coach from Connecticut, USA. She loves to write about healing, wholeness, mental health, self-love, and self-compassion. She believes in the infinite worth of each individual, and that even just one person rooting for you can make a big difference. She hopes her writing will remind people that healing is possible, that following their heart is courageous, that authenticity is beautiful, and that they are not alone. You can find her writing on Instagram at @dearbeautifulfriend, and her poetry prints and more on Etsy at dearbeautifulfriend.

Instagram: @dearbeautifulfriend
Website: linktr.ee/dearbeautifulfriend
Etsy: dearbeautifulfriend
Email: dearbeautifulfriend@gmail.com

Made in the USA
Las Vegas, NV
29 December 2024